Contents

Acknowledgements

The authors would like to thank all those adults with dyslexia who, over the years, have asked the questions that this booklet seeks to answer. We hope that it will provide enough information to get adults with dyslexia started on the quest for further knowledge about the condition which can make life challenging for them.

We particularly want to thank those brave adults who, having experienced unemployment, have returned to study at the Career Paths for Dyslexia training course. They were most helpful at the planning stages of this booklet. Their comments, suggestions and insight were invaluable. The quotations from material which they contributed, as well as those from Derry Ann and Sam, demonstrate more clearly than any words of ours just how dyslexia affects the person. We thank them all for their generosity.

Special thanks to Emma Matthews, Mary Wafaie, Sheila Kavanagh, Margaret Doyle, Antoinette O'Reilly and Cridwynn Rawlings, who have worked for many years on the Career Paths course. They shared their experience, expertise and first-hand knowledge of overcoming dyslexia in adulthood.

Many thanks also to Don Mullan, a good friend of the Dyslexia Association, for having the courage to speak out so honestly about his own dyslexia, and allowing us to reproduce his story here.

Finally, a debt of thanks is due to all those who have worked with the Dyslexia Association in a professional or voluntary capacity over the years. Their efforts have led to a wider awareness of dyslexia. We hope this booklet will contribute to an even greater understanding of how dyslexia affects adults and the tremendous potential that exists to turn a difference into an advantage.

Introduction

This booklet is intended to give relevant information to adults who know that they have dyslexia, to those who think that they might have, and for those who have never even considered the possibility.

It is also intended for employers, managers and human resource personnel. The experience of the Dyslexia Association of Ireland over the years has proved that the need for such information exists.

Despite increased awareness, generated through media coverage, seminars and word of mouth, dyslexia, particularly as it affects adults, is still not taken seriously enough in this country.

There are thousands of Irish adults with dyslexia, many of whom are unaware that there is a recognised explanation for their continuing difficulty with literacy. There are people who have struggled for years with information processing difficulties which have seriously hindered them at school and at work. There are employers, supervisors and managers who may never have considered that dyslexia impacts on their workforce. If they think of dyslexia at all, they probably consider it a difficulty of childhood, or of those who never completed school.

Dyslexia is a complex condition, but its main effect is to make learning to read, write and spell difficult. Not impossible, just difficult. It is not caused by lack of intelligence, lack of effort or any physical or emotional problem. It is an inherited condition and so may be passed on to children or grandchildren. It is more common than is generally realised, affecting 6% to 8% of the population.

There are various theories about what causes dyslexia, but all experts agree that it arises from differences in the brain which affect how the brain processes information. It must be stressed that dyslexia is a 'difference', not a disease or a defect. Yet it is a very important difference, because it has implications for many aspects of the dyslexic person's life. In the past when literacy was neither vital to daily life nor very valued, having dyslexia was not a drawback.
In the future, it may well be that developments in information technology will make literacy, as we know it, irrelevant. Then, the person with dyslexia will not be at a disadvantage at all. Possibly, with good creative, visual and problem solving skills, they will have a distinct advantage. However, in today's society, people with dyslexia are in an unenviable position. Not only is work, travel and leisure dominated by the written word, but skill in planning, organisation and time management are more important than ever before. Completing tasks to a time schedule, absorbing new information quickly and working under pressure are requirements of every workplace. None of these come easily to the person with dyslexia.

An area which is easily overlooked is the effect which dyslexia can have on social and family life. Years of battling with a world which demands that they engage every day with the very things they find most difficult can cause anger and frustration in adults with dyslexia. This can sometimes make them uncomfortable people to live or work with and can have implications for personal and family relationships.

The number of people involved; those with dyslexia, their families, friends and work colleagues, makes it imperative that a greater understanding is developed of how dyslexia affects adults, of the challenges they face and of the many ways in which these can be overcome and turned into solid achievement.

The first two chapters of this book provide a basic introduction to dyslexia and other specific learning difficulties. Chapter 3 provides information on how to obtain an assessment so that an accurate diagnosis of the condition can be made. Chapter 4 lists some options for moving forward, while Chapter 5 gives more detailed information on dyslexia. Chapters 6 and 7 deal with how dyslexia affects adults socially, while studying and in the workplace and suggests some strategies for coping with it. Chapter 8 offers information for employers. Finally, Chapter 9 provides information on resources and technology. Information on the Dyslexia Association is contained in Appendix A, and references and resources are listed in Appendix B.

But first – a story. Read the very personal account of how dyslexia affected one man's life.

"Breaking Free From the Lie" by Don Mullan.

"From the first day I went to school I was in trouble with reading.

The year was 1961. It was a year that saw Soviet cosmonaut, Yuri Gagarin, become the first man in space and the year when newly elected John F. Kennedy promised the American people that they would win the race to the moon. It was also the start of the decade when scientists and educators began to realise that specific learning disabilities, such as reading complications caused by dyslexia, weren't necessarily linked to a child's IQ.

Unfortunately, for my generation, it would take a couple of decades more before their discoveries and innovative recommendations began to filter into the education system.

I do not hold any bitterness towards my primary or secondary school teachers. They were as ignorant as their pupils about dyslexia and its manifestations. With little awareness teachers engaged in a very flawed assessment process which assumed that reading ability was a barometer for measuring a child's intelligence. It was the beginning of a self-fulfilling prophecy that left an indelible mark of self-doubt on pupils who, like me, are dyslexic and which haunts legions of my generation to this day.

I went to primary school in Derry. It was essentially a filter school, preparing pupils for a horrendous final examination called the Eleven-Plus. Those who passed were given a passport to the more academically inclined St. Columb's College, where university beckoned. Those who 'failed' were sent to a vocational secondary school where expectations led pupils generally towards factory work and the service industries.

From first grade to my final year at primary school I fluctuated between the last two rows on the teacher's left. Those to the teacher's right were considered to be the more intelligent and, inevitably, the best readers. As a child I very quickly learned my place in the stratosphere of intellectual giftedness. The system religiously adhered to a doctrine of predestination. There were some people born 'smart' and some born 'slow.' I happened to be in the latter. That's the way it was and there wasn't a lot I, or anyone associated with me, could do about it.

I still cringe at the thought of reading out loud before the class. Even though I would have spent hours the evening before with my mother learning the assigned homework pages from our reading book, 'Dick and Dora' the words presented themselves as a foreign language when I was in class.

The assumption, of course, was that my reading difficulties were simply due to a lack of grey matter. It was not a system that, unlike today, values the individuality and uniqueness of the child. School was not a fun place to be. Learning was a chore, not a joy. Punishment for 'failure' reinforced the low self-esteem that characterises the dyslexic child. Struggling to read out loud, in the presence of other children, who appeared to effortlessly excel, simply confirmed one's sense of stupidity. 'Dunce' was a word, thrown like a rotten egg in the playground, which shattered one's confidence and splattered one's self-image with negativity.

I learned in those early days the inherent power of words to wound, or heal, especially when uttered by an adult. Teachers should never underestimate how a throw away remark, either negative or positive, can leave an indelible mark. There are two teachers, in particular, who taught me the nobility and horror of the teaching profession at primary level.

My favourite teacher was Master Flood. He had a compassionate and caring nature which I recall with gratitude and respect almost four decades later. There was never a sense of frustration or favouritism. When his eyes engaged you, you knew you were looking at an adult who liked and valued you. Forty years later I do not recall any words spoken by John Flood. I only recall kindness.

I had just turned eleven in my final year at Primary School when our class was placed with Master G whose task it was to prepare us for the Eleven Plus examination. We had him for no more than three weeks but his influence stayed with me for as many decades. I learned from him that the average intelligence quotient was measured at 100. In the pre-examination tests I was scoring an average of 76-84, reinforcing an already wounded self-image.

After our two or three weeks with Master G he drew up a list of those whom he considered capable of passing the examination. He duly read it aloud. He then asked if there was anyone else in the class whose name was not on the list but who wanted to sit the exam. I raised my hand.

With fixed gaze he looked at me. Then with a pitying smirk, he lowered his head and spoke the words, "You've no chance!" They were uttered with caustic cynicism and the laugher of my classmates, in response, indelibly recorded his words in my mind. Those words played over and over and over again, filling me with immense insecurities and self-doubt for almost thirty years. I still cringe with the memory of the humiliation they visited upon me at that moment."

Twenty-seven years later, Don Mullan was diagnosed as having dyslexia. Furthermore, a psycho-educational assessment confirmed that far from being 'slow', Don's IQ was within the top 5% of the population. Don recalls:

"As the implications of the report began to sink in, the words "you've no chance" echoed in my head. However, they no longer conjured feelings of self-doubt and despondency, but a volcano of rage. My first thought was for the teacher who spoke them.

I needed to confront him with the decades of damage he had done and the potential he had crushed."

Fortunately, Don Mullan overcame his anger. He focused his energy instead on coping with his dyslexia. He undertook challenges in his work which he had not had the courage to tackle previously. Being diagnosed with dyslexia was akin to the life changing revelation of Saul on the road to Damascus. He says:

"The most liberating insight is knowing that my reading difficulties, including my perpetual struggle with spelling and grammar, have little to do with intelligence. My mind works in a different way and, thankfully, I have been blessed with a creative imagination that never leaves me bored.

We all have strengths and weaknesses. We all have different gifts to share and much to learn. I've stopped beating myself up because I can't do certain things which I see others do with little effort. I have learned to celebrate the success of others and know that whatever success I have achieved is due, in no small measure, to the goodness, support and encouragement of others. Being dyslexic has taught me that sharing and caring is core to human happiness and fulfilment.

So, I am not ashamed to publicly declare that I am dyslexic. I do so in the knowledge that there are probably legions of my generation who have accepted the lie that their reading difficulties are due to a deficiency in intellectual attributes. I went through my adolescence and early adulthood doubting my intellectual capabilities. Discovering that I am dyslexic dispelled the lie and set me on a road to new and unimagined adventures. I have no doubt that there are thousands of adults who are underachieving and who are not reaching their full potential because, as children, they accepted, as a supreme truth, that lie.

Discovering that I am dyslexic quite literally set me free from it."

The full text of Don Mullan's biographical piece "Breaking free from the Lie" can be found on **www.dyslexia.ie/conference2004.htm.**

Don Mullan is the best-selling author of *'Eyewitness Bloody Sunday'.*
This book was a major catalyst in the re-opening of the Bloody Sunday Inquiry by Tony Blair in 1998. The book also inspired the making of the award-winning film *Bloody Sunday* which was coproduced by Mullan.

Don Mullan is a writer and journalist with an international reputation. His contribution to human rights was acknowledged by the International League for Human Rights at the United Nations in 2002 when he was awarded their *Defenders of Human Dignity Award.*

Chapter 1
What is Dyslexia?

Two adults with dyslexia were asked what dyslexia means to them.
This is what they said:

Sam (Diagnosed with dyslexia in primary school):

"Dyslexia would be no big deal if people only understood it. You can learn to handle it but you must get help, and you have to keep working at it. The annoying thing for me is how some people react. It can take me longer to get the hang of something new and there are some things, like maths, that I don't get at all.

Other things I can understand immediately and I'd say I have a wider knowledge in a lot of areas than most people. But I can get confused. I can miss a point or forget something important.

Then people react as if you are the village idiot. It used to make me angry when teachers carried on as if I was stupid because I found something difficult that other people found easy. As an adult it is much easier because now I won't take that anymore."

Derry Ann (Diagnosed as an adult):

"Dyslexia is part of me. That is what I am. Take it
or leave it. It makes me do things differently.
It helps me to see things that other people don't.
I can find solutions, work my way round situations
and think myself through difficulties. School was
very hard for me. Reading and spelling were so
difficult. No matter how hard I tried I just could not
remember what I had learned. It was an unhappy
time, nobody understood and I didn't understand
myself.

Since I was diagnosed as having dyslexia the
world has fallen into place for me and I have
achieved more than I ever thought possible
because I now know what caused my difficulties.
Now I believe in myself and follow my own
instincts, develop my own strengths and learn by
doing, which is what suits me best."

For Sam and Derry Ann dyslexia is a very personal
issue. Problems they experienced were caused not just
by their dyslexia, but by the lack of understanding in
the people they met. While awareness of dyslexia has
increased greatly in recent years, there is still a long
way to go until dyslexia is seen not merely as a
difficulty, but as a difference. It is a different way of
thinking, a different way of seeing things, a different
way of processing information. It's a difference
which could, and should, be appreciated for its positive
aspects.

Defining Dyslexia

Over the years since dyslexia was first written about, there have been numerous definitions and descriptions of what it is and how it can be identified. At first it was described as word blindness, then as *strephosymbolia,* meaning a *twisting of symbols* and eventually as dyslexia. The word dyslexia comes from the Greek *dus/dys* meaning bad or *difficult* and lexis meaning *word, vocabulary* or *language.*

Dyslexia can be written about in terms of how one learns to read and write; or in terms of subtle differences in the way the brain responds to the written word. These differences make it more than usually difficult to learn to read, write and, sometimes, deal with numbers.

On the other side, it is documented that people with dyslexia can be more advanced in the ways they see, understand and process nonverbal information and can be very creative and novel in problemsolving.

Dyslexia is an all-embracing term. It describes a complex of processing activities and abilities which come into play when one needs to read and write. These processes and abilities are also likely to affect how one learns, organises a task and deals with many everyday tasks. One lives with dyslexia. As it is not a medical problem it cannot be cured. As it is genetic it does not go away. The person with dyslexia can adapt and find new ways to deal with information processing, thus getting around the original difficulties, and often exploiting their strengths to do this.

Dyslexia can occur at different degrees of difficulty, mild to severe. Because there are a number of different 'indicators' there may be different combinations of difficulties from person to person: in any group of people with dyslexia there are a range of abilities and difficulties both within the individual and between the individuals. Some will have greater difficulty. Some will have greater ability. Usually the reading and writing delay is quite unexpected, given the individual's alertness and good ability in other aspects of learning.

When the Task Force on Dyslexia, set up by the Minister for Education and Science, published its Report in July 2001, it defined dyslexia as follows:

"Dyslexia is manifested in a continuum of specific learning difficulties related to the acquisition of basic skills in reading, spelling and/or writing, such difficulties being unexpected in relation to an individual's other abilities and educational experiences. Dyslexia can be described at the neurological, cognitive and behavioural levels. It is typically characterised by inefficient information processing, including difficulties in phonological processing, working memory, rapid naming and automaticity of basic skills. Difficulties in organisation, sequencing and motor skills may also be present."

Academic definitions of dyslexia generally present it in terms of the difficulties it causes. While this approach is often criticised by people with dyslexia it has to be admitted that in today's society, which is so dependent on the written word, dyslexia does indeed cause problems. The most widely recognised are:

- Unexpected difficulty with literacy and numeracy.
- Difficulties in recognising the sound structures of a language (phonological difficulties).
- Poor working memory, i.e. retaining information long enough to be able to do something with it such as calculate how much change you should get back, connect paragraph with paragraph of what you have read.
- Delay in finding the right word quickly when you need it, e.g. naming an object/experience accurately, or relating the symbols you see on the page with the word you know in your head.
- Delay in becoming automatic in a skill, particularly in the skills of reading and spelling.

Main Characteristics/Indicators of Dyslexia
The ways in which dyslexia has an impact on day-to-day living tend to change over the years. In primary school the focus is on learning to read, write and spell. The main difficulties experienced will be in matching sounds of words with patterns of letters and remembering which direction letters face. Difficulties with motor co-ordination, memory and attention will also be noted.

In secondary school the student must read to learn. The challenge, therefore, is to be able to deal with the range of subjects, the volume of reading and writing required and to prepare for and manage timed examinations.

In adult life reading and writing still present difficulties but so do planning, organising, speed of processing, memory and sometimes clumsiness. Slower processing of auditory and visual information, difficulty with working memory, phonological difficulty and poor spelling are aspects of dyslexia which are constant and which do not go away when one leaves school. It may still be hard to read fluently when reading aloud. Most adults with dyslexia have to use memos and calculators and a host of strategies to remind them of tasks to be done, names and numbers to be remembered and directions to be followed. Many continue to have difficulty attending to a long lecture or speech. Listening and taking notes at the same time may be very difficult. They can have difficulty in remembering names, addresses or telephone numbers. Difficulties in managing time and organising tasks are aspects of work and home life which need constant attention.

However, the adult with dyslexia may also have developed other learning skills and characteristics that stand them in good stead. Many adults with dyslexia are very thorough, because they leave nothing to chance. They plan carefully because they have to be prepared. Having had to work much harder than their peers while at school or college, they develop the ability to apply themselves to a task and persevere despite setbacks. Having overcome a lot of difficulties in acquiring skills which most people learn to do automatically, or with relative ease, they are more likely to believe in their own ability to achieve their goals.

Below are lists of indicators which may show that a dyslexic difficulty is present. **When looking at the lists of indicators, remember the following:**
- No person will have all the indicators.
- Many people will have several of the indicators.
- Some indicators are more common than others.
- The number of indicators observed does not indicate whether the dyslexia is mild, moderate or severe.
- Everyone has strengths and weaknesses so people who do not have dyslexia will relate to a few of the signs. People who have dyslexia will tend to relate to a significant number of the following indicators.

Indicators of a possible learning difficulty arising from dyslexia in adults:

- ✓ Difficulty with reading aloud.
- ✓ Difficulty with reading unfamiliar material.
- ✓ Tendency to mispronounce or misread words.
- ✓ Slow pace of reading.
- ✓ Reading for information only, not for pleasure.
- ✓ Understanding more easily when listening than when reading.
- ✓ Difficulty with spelling.
- ✓ Finding it hard to visualise words, or remember the sequence of letters in a word.
- ✓ Difficulty with sentence construction and punctuation.
- ✓ Difficulty putting information on paper.
- ✓ Difficulty in spotting mistakes made in written work.
- ✓ Finding it easier to express thoughts in words than in writing.
- ✓ Underachieving at school, particularly in exams.
- ✓ Having immature or ill formed handwriting.
- ✓ Tendency to be clumsy and uncoordinated.
- ✓ Confusing left and right.
- ✓ Finding it hard to remember things in sequence.
- ✓ Difficulty in remembering new information or new names.
- ✓ Getting phone messages wrong.
- ✓ Confusion with times and dates and appointments.
- ✓ Getting phone numbers wrong by perhaps reversing digits.

- ✓ Making 'silly' mistakes in calculations.
- ✓ Having 'good' days and 'bad' days.
- ✓ Poor short-term memory.
- ✓ Having close family members with dyslexia.

An adult who suspects that s/he may have dyslexia and who finds they experience many of the difficulties listed above, might be well advised to seek a full psycho-educational assessment. (See chapter 3 for further information on assessment.)

Chapter 2
Dyslexia/Specific
Learning Disability (SLD)

Many people are confused about the terms used to describe dyslexia.

Should it more properly be called 'specific learning disability', 'specific learning difficulty', or even 'learning style difference'? How do you differentiate between dyslexia and the other specific learning disabilities? And how do you define conditions like dyscalculia?

Specific learning disability is an umbrella term. Since the 1990s it has been used to describe a number of specific, as distinct from general learning disabilities. Specific difficulties only affect certain aspects of learning. General learning difficulties affect every aspect of learning.

Dyslexia is only one specific learning disability. Others are:

- Dyscalculia.
- Dyspraxia.
- Attention Deficit Disorder (with or without Hyperactivity).
- Asperger's Syndrome.

These conditions often carry over into adulthood and have profound implications for students and workers. While each of these is distinct from the other it is recognised that a person with dyslexia can also show signs of inattention, like the person with Attention Deficit Disorder; or have difficulty with maths, like the person with dyscalculia; or be clumsy, like the person with dyspraxia. There does seem to be an overlap between the Specific Learning Difficulties in many cases.

Dyscalculia

It is reckoned that over 50% of people with dyslexia have problems with mathematics. In extreme cases this difficulty is called dyscalculia. Dyscalculia results in difficulty with understanding, remembering or manipulating numbers and number facts. It can also cause problems with estimating measurements, the passing of time and spatial reasoning. It can sometimes be true that people who have difficulties with fairly simple arithmetic do not have any problems with more abstract mathematical concepts. Dyscalculia is a much less researched disability than dyslexia and it is likely that in the coming years much more will be revealed about the condition.

Sam, who experiences great difficulty with maths, says:

"Maths means nothing to me. I am not interested. I can handle money, pay bills and deal with practical things. I am fine when sums are even, like €3.50 from €5.00 but when it's a case of €2.36 and €1.43 I get confused. I just can't understand abstract concepts like algebra. When I see 3x + 2y I just switch off. I've never worked out my income tax and things like that. I just accept my payslip."

For further information read "Dealing with Dyscalculia: Sum Hope 2" by Steve Chinn (2007)
ISBN 978-0285637986.

Dyspraxia
The aspects of Dyspraxia most likely to cause problems for adults are lack of fine motor co-ordination (which can result in illegible handwriting), clumsiness, sensitivity to noise and changing light, limited concentration and difficulty following instructions. Learning to drive a car, to dance, play a musical instrument or to play ball games can all be difficult. Even basic everyday activities like eating neatly, painting finger nails or putting on mascara could be affected. Many of the workplace problems which arise from dyspraxia are very similar to those caused by dyslexia and the two are frequently confused. People with dyspraxia often have dyslexic type difficulties and the two conditions are very closely linked. The following books are recommended for those seeking more information on dyspraxia:

- Developmental Dyspraxia – by M. Portwood, 1999, ISBN 978-1853469886.
- Living with Dyspraxia – by M. Colley, 2006, ISBN 978-1843104520.

The Dyspraxia Association of Ireland also offers information, advice and support. Tel. 01 4045530. www.dyspraxiaireland.com.

Attention Deficit Hyperactivity Disorders (ADD/ADHD)

ADD/ADHD describes a condition where the person has more than usual difficulty maintaining attention for any length of time and is highly distractible, disorganised and forgetful.

A rather weary woman once described her hyperactive husband as being:

"Like the Duracell bunny, always on the go, bouncing around the place, full of bright ideas and suggestions but it's left to me to pick up the pieces."

The person may take up new ideas very enthusiastically, but lose interest just as quickly. Routine tasks may be unattractive and putting things on the 'long finger' is a way of life. In recent years it has been acknowledged that ADD can exist with hyperactivity, or without it, but in either case the core difficulty is with ability to control attention.

A great deal of research has been done in the United States on this topic.

Dr. Lynn Weiss, author of "ADD on the Job" identifies three types of ADD personality which she calls: **Outwardly Expressive; Inwardly Directed and Highly Structured.**

The Outwardly Expressive person will be both verbally and physically hyperactive, impulsive and outgoing, taking on huge projects which may never be completed.

The Inwardly Directed she describes as restless dreamers who are artistic, creative people, who think rather than do. These are the people usually diagnosed as having Attention Deficit Disorder without Hyperactivity.

The Highly Structured are controlling and hyper focused. If the structured environment in which they need to work is not provided, life becomes difficult for everyone, but in the right circumstances they work extremely efficiently.

Dr. Weiss offers practical advice for dealing with ADD/ADHD in the workplace. She describes it, in effect, as a double edged sword. Like dyslexia it is genetic and it results in a different style of thinking. People with ADD can be very creative and intuitive. Those with ADHD can be extremely energetic and productive if channeled correctly. Both these conditions can be accommodated in the workplace and utilized to good effect.

For further information read "ADD on the Job: Making Your ADD Work for You" by L. Weiss (1996), ISBN 978-0878339174.

Information, advice and support is available from the HADD Family Support Group, Tel. 01 874 8349. www.hadd.ie.

Asperger's Syndrome
The term Asperger's Syndrome came into use as recently as 1983, in a paper published by Burgoine and Wing which describes the features that are considered to characterise the disability. In the 1940s a Viennese paediatrician, Hans Asperger, had already identified these, hence the name. Asperger's Syndrome is usually classified under the Autistic Spectrum Disorders.

The following are the core features of Asperger's Syndrome:
- Lack of empathy.
- Poor ability to form friendships.
- One-sided conversations.
- Intense absorption in a special interest.
- Poor verbal communication.
- Odd postures and clumsy movements.

It should be remembered that the presence of any one or any cluster of these features do not in themselves indicate Asperger's Disorder, for example, poor communication skills, and consequently poor ability to hold a two-sided conversation, may be caused by a language disorder. The only way to get a true diagnosis is to have an appropriate assessment which is wide-ranging and thorough.

People with Asperger's Syndrome are often quite academic and may function well in a highly structured situation. While school life may suit them, the challenge of the workplace can be greater, particularly if flexibility and adaptability are required.

For further information read – "The Asperger Social Guide" – by G. Edmonds and D. Worton, 2006, Chapman Educational Publishing.
ISBN 978-1412920247.

Information, advice and support is available from Aspire, the Asperger Syndrome Association,
Tel. 01 878 0027.
www.aspire-irl.org

Chapter 3
Psycho-Educational Assessment

The only way in which dyslexia can be positively identified in an adult is by carrying out a thorough psycho-educational assessment. There are four stages in a person's quest to have his/her dyslexia identified according to McLoughlin, Fitzgibbon and Young (1994). These are:
1. Information gathering.
2. Psychological testing and diagnosis.
3. Developing an understanding of dyslexia.
4. Taking action.

Information Gathering
This can be more difficult than one would imagine. Obviously it is necessary to know about a condition in order to suspect that one might have it. Many adults who have dyslexia have never even heard the word and have no idea of how it affects learning. They are, therefore, unlikely to seek assessment unless encouraged by someone who knows about the condition. There is a great deal which can be done to help adults with dyslexia, both in terms of formal teaching and self-help techniques. Again, information about the possibilities of further action after assessment needs to be available.

The internet has made information gathering much simpler for those of the community who use computers, but many people, particularly those with literacy difficulties are not regular users. The Dyslexia Association of Ireland has a free public information service. The phone number is 01 6790276 and anyone may call during normal office hours. The website is **www.dyslexia.ie.**

Psychological Testing and Diagnosis
The second step, psychological testing, is more difficult. Assessment is costly, difficult to obtain and not everyone believes that it is essential. Psycho-educational assessment is carried out by a psychologist and can range in cost from €400 to €700. There is no state provision for adults, even for those who are unemployed or who have a medical card. It can also be hard to locate a suitably qualified psychologist and waiting lists tend to be long.

The Dyslexia Association of Ireland has been carrying out assessments for adults for over 30 years. The Association is able to fund some assessments for adults who would otherwise be unable to have an assessment, i.e. people on social welfare or low-income families. This facility depends on funding from the Department of Education and Science but this funding is not guaranteed from year to year. Therefore, the association also relies heavily on fund raising to supplement government funding for this purpose.

Is Assessment Necessary?

It is important to discover just why a learning difficulty exists, because unless you know the precise nature of the problem, it is not going to be possible to deal with it effectively. Psycho-educational assessment for adults is about pinpointing the difficulty and advising on remediation. It is not about putting a label on the person. A diagnosis of lung cancer does not create a label. Instead it gives medical experts the information they need to prescribe suitable treatment. Likewise, a diagnosis of dyslexia enables a person to begin the process of dealing with the condition. It is often an enormous relief for adults, who have felt stupid and inadequate all through life, to realise that they have an identifiable difficulty. In all fairness, adults with dyslexia are entitled to this knowledge about themselves. **Knowledge empowers and knowing about a condition is the first step towards managing it.**

The technology now exists to carry out screening and certain assessment procedures on computer. Screening tests, whether paper or computer based, can be a valuable starting point, but they do not provide comprehensive information and a basis for future action. Computer based assessments, however sophisticated, lack the human element. The assessing psychologist needs to take the person's medical and educational history, as well as other environmental factors into account before a reliable conclusion can be reached. Besides, there will inevitably be many issues for the newly diagnosed adult to deal with; regret for wasted years, anger at past treatment in school or at work or fear of the future.

These are best handled in a professional way by a trained psychologist.

Only a psychologist may carry out the necessary psychometric testing. McLoughlin et al (1994) say:

> "The accurate diagnosis of dyslexia requires the measurement of general ability and working memory. Any procedure that fails to incorporate appropriate cognitive tests is likely to produce both false positives and false negatives."

The authors add that the appropriate assessment of intelligence is one of the most crucial factors in diagnosis. This stands to reason. There are many reasons why adults have literacy difficulties and dyslexia is only one of them. While the effects of literacy difficulties are similar, the causes are very different. The results of the International Adult Literacy Survey, published in 1997, indicated that 25% of Irish adults had pronounced literacy problems. The reasons for these difficulties could be early school leaving, irregular school attendance, overcrowded classrooms, lack of family support for learning, low academic ability or dyslexia. If the latter two factors are confused, as they often were in the schoolrooms of the past, the result can be disastrous.

The Assessment Process

The reason why a person who suspects they may have dyslexia seeks a psycho-educational assessment is to determine whether they do indeed have a dyslexic-type difficulty, the nature and extent of the problem and how they can be helped to cope. The focus of the assessment, therefore, is on finding out how the person learns and helping them to use their best learning channels. Its aim is positive – to put the person in the driving seat in relation to their own lives.

The psycho-educational assessment begins with a review of the person's family and school history. Areas of difficulty encountered are listed and family incidence of dyslexia is noted. Some standard tests are used to assess how the individual copes with academic learning. This is the I.Q. test. It is carried out, not to pinpoint a score on a graph, but to look at how the person tackles different tasks and in the relative strengths they show. Reading, writing and spelling skills are also looked at, with a view to identifying problem areas and suggesting strategies to overcome difficulties.

A psycho-educational assessment is not an exam. It is not intended to put the individual under stress and it is not possible to 'fail' such an assessment. While many people approach an assessment with the same anxiety as they would a driving test, others see it as their chance to find out just why they have found some aspects of learning difficult. The procedure usually takes around three hours and will probably include discussion on the results of the assessment and advice on future action.

The psychologist should provide an adult with a written report on the findings of the assessment. Sometimes this report is written in very technical language and may be difficult to understand. It may be necessary to contact the psychologist to discuss the actual implications of the assessment and of the information contained in the report. It should be remembered that an assessment report has to contain precise and technical information which will be needed by an educational institution, or a tutor. It also needs to explain the findings in a way which can be understood by the lay person. It is not easy to meet both these needs in one document. The adult with dyslexia should be prepared to read the report several times, and to go back to it again over the months or years as their knowledge of dyslexia grows. A good tip is to look at what the report has to say about where the individual's strengths lie, because these are the key to successful learning.

Adults who are recently diagnosed may also need to take on board and deal with any feelings of anger or frustration which the assessment process aroused. Sometimes counselling by an appropriate professional person may be necessary.

It is really important that the results and implications of assessment are fully explained to the individual. Adults who understand their own profile of learning strengths and weaknesses will be much more aware of their own preferred learning style. Learning styles are explained in Chapter 5, while self-help strategies are offered in Chapter 6.

Knowledge of strengths and personal learning styles can also help an individual to make the best possible career choice. Ideally one should choose a career which taps into their stronger abilities and aptitudes, as opposed to a career which places huge demands on their weaker skills.

Chapter 4
Taking Action

It is very important to have a full diagnosis of dyslexia and to find out just what causes specific difficulties in the area of literacy. It is equally important to know what can be done to improve matters. Each person will have different learning strengths and weaknesses. Each personal situation will differ. Some will have greater difficulty than others. Some will have money available with which to buy specialized teaching help or technology. Some will not. Some employers will be understanding of a dyslexic type difficulty and prepared to make adjustments in the workplace. Some will not.

So, what are the possible next steps for an adult diagnosed with dyslexia?

1. Tuition with a specifically trained teacher.
2. Full-time study.
3. Understanding how dyslexia affects them.
4. Self-help techniques to overcome the difficulties.
5. Use of information technology.

Individual Tuition

Ideally, an adult with dyslexia should work with a specifically trained teacher who uses the information provided by a thorough psychoeducational assessment to devise an effective teaching programme.

Best results are obtained when teaching is provided on an intensive and consistent basis. Successfully tutoring adults with dyslexia requires considerable skill and training. The Dyslexia Association of Ireland maintains a list of such teachers and this is available to members. Tutors work at all levels. Some will take on students with very severe literacy difficulties. Others are quite happy to work with students engaged in post-graduate studies. Tutors respond to the individual needs of the student and the important thing is to match student and tutor so that a good working relationship develops.

Fees are in the range of €35 to €50 per hour. Limited funding may be available from the Dyslexia Association for those unable to meet these fees, i.e. adults who are on social welfare, or where family income is low.

Tuition may also be obtained through local adult literacy services, which now have some tutors experienced in working with adults with dyslexia. Information can be obtained from the National Adult Literacy Agency, or from local Vocational Education Committees.

Full-time Courses

A full-time course for unemployed adults with dyslexia is sponsored by the Dyslexia Association and administered by FÁS. This course, which is the only one of its kind in Ireland so far, is located in Celbridge, Co. Kildare. It has been running since 1998 and in that time has helped hundreds of adults to tackle long-standing literacy difficulties and move on to work or further study.

A former student, Brendan, writes:

"I found the experience of returning to learning to be very positive and rewarding, and I really relished the classroom atmosphere and the various discussions that take place there.
This course reintroduced me to learning, helping me to help myself in finding out where my problem lay."

Brendan is now in full-time third level education.

Ciaran, like many others who attend the Career Paths course found school life very difficult. He says "it was hell on earth. I spent my school days in misery". He left school after Junior Cert and apprenticed as a plumber, but his working life had its problems too.

"I quickly realised that my dyslexia was not just affecting my school work but it was affecting me doing my job. I started to find that I had to go back and check everything twice. I found it hard to read the measuring tape. It was unlucky that I worked for a big company because I was apprenticed with one person for a while. When they saw that I was not up to scratch they would recommend to the boss that I go working with someone else in the company."

Ciaran eventually lost his job and was unemployed for almost a year. He was at 'rock bottom' when he enrolled on the course. Having given up school at age 15 he found it strange to be back in a class room with a pen and paper. He persevered and as he says …

"I started to see a big improvement in literacy and along with personal development I found my confidence lifting and I am somewhere for the first time where I am not feeling anxious, nervous and all of the other bad feelings that go along with dyslexia. My life is much improved. I will finish my time in the Career Path centre where I am concentrating on getting ready for college and I hope to take a course in Media Studies."

Information about the Career Paths course is available from:

- Career Paths Course, Office No. 1, The Mill, Celbridge, Co. Kildare. Tel. 01 627 0805.

- Dyslexia Association. Tel. 01 679 0276 www.dyslexia.ie

- Any FÁS office. Course Code AT58F.

Further Study
Many adults are motivated to have a psycho-educational assessment when they plan to take further courses.
Conversely, many adults decide to return to education when they have had an assessment and become aware of their own potential.

Whatever the motivation, it is very encouraging to note the variety of help and support which is now available to students with dyslexia in further education.

Most colleges and educational bodies now recognise dyslexia as a specific learning disability and put arrangements in place to cater for students. Proof of the existence of a specific learning disability, in the form of an up-to-date and comprehensive psycho-educational assessment is usually required. As provisions vary from one college or institute to another, it is advisable to contact the Disability Support Office of an individual organisation to check what accommodations are put in place. It may also be necessary for the student to be very active in ensuring that the support promised is received, as resources are limited and sometimes the promised support does not translate into help on the ground.

Accommodations provided may include: a more flexible approach to entry requirements to a particular course; there may be support available by provision of specialised tuition, or by provision of information technology. In many universities and colleges, lecture notes may be made available, even before the lecture and may be available on internet or intranet afterwards. Extra time may be given when sitting examinations; use of a dictaphone or computer may be allowed; an extension of deadlines for the completion of essays or written projects may be negotiated and in some cases examiners are prepared to consider oral answers to supplement written answers to examination questions.

Gaining qualifications
For the adult who wants to gain qualifications which will be useful in terms of employment, there are many possibilities. It is possible to study by day or by night or on-line. In order to make an informed decision about how worthwhile a course is, it is necessary to understand the National Framework of Qualifications (www.nfq.ie). This framework was introduced in 2003. It is a system of ten levels that incorporates awards made for all kinds of learning, wherever it happens. The NFQ, through its ten levels, provides a means of comparing and contrasting national and international education and training qualifications. It makes it easier for people to explain what qualifications they hold or are studying for. This is very important when considering further learning or applying for a job abroad. It helps learners to plan their education and training and it helps employers to identify the qualifications they require.

School qualifications awarded by the State Examinations Commission, further education and training qualifications awarded by FETAC and higher education and training qualifications awarded by HETAC, Dublin Institute of Technology (DIT), other institutes of technology and the universities all slot into this framework. The levels which might be of interest to adults returning to education are as follows:

Level	Examples of courses at this level
Level 3	Junior Certificate.
Level 4	Leaving Certificate and other courses.
Level 5	Leaving Certificate and PLCs.
Level 6	Higher Certificate Courses in CAO.
Level 7	CAO Ordinary Degree.
Level 8	CAO Honours Degree.
Level 9	Masters Degree.
Level 10	Doctorate (PhD).

Choosing Courses

There are different routes and structures to obtaining new qualifications. Qualifications can be offered in a variety of ways from distance learning, to evening courses to full time courses. Below are a number of websites which might help the person thinking of returning to education and learning. Some sites include career interest assessment which might be helpful in deciding which course to pursue.

www.nightcourses.com
This site gives a database and search facility to look for a night course.

www.aontas.com
The National Adult Learning Organisation promotes a learning society through the provision of a comprehensive system of adult learning and education which is accessible to and inclusive to all. It provides a list of websites which provide on-line distance learning among other valuable information.

www.oscail.ie
Oscail, the National Distance Education Centre of Ireland, offers the opportunity to receive Irish university qualifications through distance learning.

www.learningpoint.ie
This site is a one stop shop for training and development for staff and volunteers working in community and voluntary organisations in Ireland.

www.eveningcourses.ie
Website for evening courses.

www.daycourses.ie
Website for day courses.

www.qualifax.ie
This site is the National Database for third level and further education courses in Ireland. Qualifax is a one stop shop for information on courses for guidance counsellors and students. Included are links to colleges and other education/training organisations. It includes an extensive list of careers as well as the definitive calendar of career events and an interest assessment to assist prospective students in making choices.

www.ncirl.ie
The website for the National College of Ireland provided details of distance learning, part-time and evening courses.

www.open.ac.uk
The Open University offers 360 undergraduate and post-graduate courses and is one of the biggest providers of distance learning.

www.careersportal.ie
This is an Irish resource dedicated to those who want to plan their career. The site includes a self assessment questionnaire, information on popular career categories, a database of careers and a course finder facility.

www.careerdirections.ie
This site includes a database on careers as well as a career interest assessment.

www.skillsireland.ie
This is a Government website. It includes advice to the Government on the current and future skills needed for the Irish economy.

Bank of Ireland Millennium Scholar's Trust. This trust is applied to the creation of scholarships for people of talent and ability who due to economic circumstances or other barriers such as disability, have been unable to reach their full potential. This and other scholarships are available from many colleges.

Chapter 5
Understanding Dyslexia

The most positive result of a psycho-educational assessment for an adult is often the validation which it provides. Self-esteem and selfconfidence are likely to be very badly affected by adverse school experiences and failure to reach potential in the workplace. A positive assessment often provides the encouragement necessary to go for job promotion or to take on further study. Derry Ann is typical of many adults who had dyslexia diagnosed in adulthood. She found the process helped her to understand why she had experienced learning difficulties. It removed the guilt she had felt that somehow she had been to blame for her difficulties. It encouraged her to explore her own potential.

The first thing Derry Ann did was to learn everything she could about dyslexia.

"I joined the Dyslexia Association. I read every bit of literature I could find. I attended conferences and I talked to other people. I was a woman on a mission. The more I learned the stronger I became. I felt that now I could hold my head up and say to anyone "I have dyslexia, I am not stupid". I realized that I am perfectly entitled to have my own way of learning. For example, if I get new equipment I will ask someone to show me how it works and then I'll practice till I get it right. I know there's no point in sitting down to read a manual of instruction. I don't feel bad about that. I will help anyone else who has a problem if I can, and I don't mind asking other people for help. I don't try to hide anymore."

How much dyslexia affects a person's life depends on many factors: the age at which the condition was diagnosed, the degree of severity, the ability of the individual, the type and quality of support received – both educational and social, the job or career chosen and even the personality of the individual.

Some people are lucky enough to have had their dyslexia identified as children and to have received support through their school years.
They have had an opportunity to understand their own learning difficulties and to take them into account when planning further education or choosing a career. The fact that they have overcome basic literacy difficulties and even secured satisfactory results in examinations does not mean that they have been 'cured' of their dyslexia. Information processing difficulties, poor short term memory, auditory processing deficits or hand-eye co-ordination difficulties do not go away. A person who chose a work area where literacy was not of vital importance could find that promotion or changing work practices require them to read and write a great deal more. Another could discover that dealing with clients abroad demands second language skills which were not acquired at school. Updating computer skills,

learning to use new technology or new equipment, re-training which has to be undertaken in certain sectors of industry, can all be difficult for a person who thought that dyslexia was left behind with schooldays. If the difficulties encountered at school were severe, then the adult may well have a reluctance to re-enter a learning situation. Knowledge of dyslexia and the opportunities which are now available to support people with dyslexia might be the key to further study or work opportunity.

Living with Dyslexia
If you have recently found out that you have dyslexia or if you are now about to tackle the problem the following ideas might be helpful:

- **Find out as much as possible about your own particular situation.** Dyslexia can be mild or severe. It can affect the academically gifted, the average learner or the less able. It can be accompanied by attention and concentration problems, dyspraxia, speech and language difficulties and by anxiety conditions. It is very important to be aware of your own profile. The person who can tell you this is the psychologist who carried out the psycho-educational assessment. Don't be afraid to ask. It's your life. If you were assessed as a child and did not receive this information then consider having a new assessment and asking questions now.

- One piece of information which your psychologist may be able to give you relates to **your personal learning style.** While there are different opinions on the whole question of learning styles, the most commonly accepted styles are: Visual; Auditory and Kinaesthetic. If you identify the learning style which suits you best you will be able to develop strategies to build on your strengths and compensate for your weaknesses.

Visual Learners like to see things. They tend to think in pictures and like to have illustrations,

 charts, diagrams, graphs, mind maps and videos when they learn. It helps to rewrite notes, to put information on index cards or post-it notes and to re-create images in their minds.

Auditory Learners think in words rather than pictures. They learn best by listening and benefit from taping information and replaying it. It helps if they discuss material to be learned with others, participate in class discussions, ask questions of the teacher and even try teaching others. Reading aloud can be helpful when trying to remember information.

Kinaesthetic Learners are the 'hands-on' people.

They learn best when they can do something. Actually wiring a circuit board would be much more informative than reading a text book or listening to a lecture about it. When learning from text it helps to underline important points, use colour to highlight or make notes in the margin. Repeating information while walking can also help.

- **Take positive action.** If you were advised by the assessing psychologist to seek professional help to improve your literacy, or to support you in further study, then go ahead. The Dyslexia Association of Ireland keeps a list of qualified teachers who offer individual tuition to adults with dyslexia. The Dyslexia Association also sponsors a full-time course for adults. This is administered by FÁS. Details of the course can be found in Chapter 4. This course is a very useful means for adults who have been unemployed or working in the home to upgrade their literacy skills and acquire computer training.

- If you left school without achieving formal qualifications, **consider the possibility of going back into education.** There is a wide variety of choices – from night classes at your local college of further education to access courses for university. Have a look at the section Gaining Qualifications in Chapter 4. As an adult, with life experience and maturity, you may be surprised at your success.

- **The Adult Education Guidance Initiative** offers information, advice and guidance on a one-to-one basis for adults who wish to return to education. This valuable service is provided by the Department of Education and Science and can be accessed through the National Centre for Guidance in Education, 42-43 Prussia Street, Dublin 7. Phone: 01 8690715. Email: info@ncge.ie Website: www.ncge.ie.

- **Employers are increasingly becoming aware of dyslexia.** Once you have a diagnosis of dyslexia and a written report it is worthwhile talking to your supervisor or employer to see what support they can offer. Have a look at the suggestions in Chapter 6 and tell your employer about any that would help you.

- You may find that the **attitude of family and friends** towards you changes now that it has been established that you have dyslexia. They will realise that there is a good reason for the difficulties you may have had at school, or in work. You may also find that your own self-esteem rises and you become more confident. This is, perhaps, the most common side effect of receiving a diagnosis of dyslexia. **When your confidence reaches the level of being able to say, "I have dyslexia, so what?" you have made a major leap forward.**

- Investigate what **modern technology** can offer. There is more information on this in Chapter 9.

- **Be aware that not all of your difficulties may be the result of dyslexia.** There are other hidden learning difficulties such as attention deficit hyperactivity disorder and dyspraxia. Like dyslexia, these are life long conditions and so may affect adults. It may be necessary to consult professionals in these areas also, to get your life under control. Some people, particularly those whose learning difficulties caused distress in childhood, may find that they need professional counselling before beginning to tackle the practical task of getting help with reading and writing. You need a clear head and no other side issues which might hamper learning.

- **Be realistic about what you can achieve.** Don't beat yourself up if you make mistakes. Everybody does. The most important thing is to note the mistakes you make and see how you can avoid them in the future.

- Finally, your **own attitude towards your dyslexia will be a very significant factor.** If you believe that fate has treated you unfairly and that the world owes you a living, you are going to make your problems worse. If, on the other hand, you decide that dyslexia is not going to stand in the way of your achieving your goals and you are prepared to put in the hard work and use every strategy you know to get round, through and over the obstacles in your path, you will get there, as many others have before you.

Chapter 6
Dyslexia in the Workplace, including Self-Help Strategies.

There are certain issues which arise for people with dyslexia in the workplace which do not affect other workers. It is very important to be aware of these as the co-operation of employer and employee can often resolve issues which, if ignored, or mishandled, can cause immense trouble. This Chapter discusses dyslexia in the workplace, and includes many self help strategies to help with reading, writing and remembering.

Disclosure of a Specific Learning Disability
Adults, particularly young adults who have recently completed their education, may find that the working environment is not as supportive of people with dyslexia as third level institutions are. A great deal of help and support may be provided at third level and it is very acceptable to declare one's dyslexia. In the working world the situation is very different. A major dilemma facing young people about to enter the workforce, as well as adults moving jobs, is whether to inform prospective employers that they have dyslexia.

Very little research has been done on employer awareness of dyslexia in Ireland. What little exists bears out what Gavin Reid, says of the UK:

"It has been suggested that employers may be less sensitive to dyslexic type disabilities than they are to other, more visible disabilities".

Therefore, the job seeker who declares his/her dyslexia on application for a job is taking a gamble.

It could turn out that the employer or human resources manager is aware of dyslexia and operates a system of equal opportunity. If the applicant does get the post, it is very probable that support will be provided to facilitate the employee. If, on the other hand, an applicant does not declare dyslexia before accepting a job offer, it could be difficult to request support or facilities at a later stage.

The biggest fear that job applicants have is that if they declare their dyslexia they may never get to the interview stage, never mind getting a job offer. If an applicant decides to raise the matter of his/her dyslexia at interview stage then it is important that they present their situation positively, telling the interviewer just what they can do and the qualities they would bring to the job.

An individual who felt that he or she had been discriminated against on the basis of a disability, such as dyslexia, could consider taking a case to the Equality Tribunal. The Equality Authority can be contacted for informal information and advice on any matter relating to equality and discrimination. The phone number of the Equality Authority is 1890 245545. The website is www.equality.ie.

Organisation and Time Management at Work
If one word were to be applied to the adult with dyslexia who is having problems in the workplace, it would probably be **disorganised.** Where the words "could try harder" are often used in school reports, the adult equivalent very often is "can't get his act together". Planning and organising, setting out timetables, distinguishing between the important and the urgent, remembering appointments, passing on telephone messages from memory and meeting deadlines can be exceptionally difficult for many people with dyslexia. Many complain of a tendency to get bogged down, overwhelmed by  the workload and very stressed. There are ways round this difficulty and some are outlined below.

Initial Job Training
The initial training may be insufficient, in that a dyslexic person may not have the same learning style as other employees. Skilled and well-qualified workers have reported an absence of flexibility in the approach to training in many firms. Research has indicated that it can take a person with dyslexia longer to acquire a skill to an automatic level. Once the skill is acquired, performance may be similar or better but in pressured work situations this extra time may not be given. Awareness of the skills, as well as the difficulties, of people with dyslexia would help greatly in this area.

Information Processing
So many office workers today suffer from information overload, that the pressure on people with dyslexia can be almost unbearable.

Most adults with dyslexia who work in professional or white-collar jobs have good reading skills. They may read quite fluently and have excellent comprehension but their reading speed may be slower.
They may also need to exercise more care not to misread a word or phrase. Letters, emails, reports, journals, magazine articles, newspaper reports – the amount of reading required to keep abreast of developments is a major burden and the time it takes often eats into leisure and family time.

Similarly, when it comes to letter or report writing, editing, checking spelling and grammar, double checking figures for reversals and placement errors, managing appointment diaries and recording telephone messages, extra time is also needed. Many people with dyslexia have problems with clerical speed and accuracy, so care is essential. Sometimes speed must be sacrificed for accuracy as it can be difficult to ensure both.

While the advent of the word processor has made life easier, it has also meant that very few people now have personal secretaries. Most people must produce their own written work. It is no longer sufficient to be a good engineer, one must also be able to write a clear and properly spelled report and perform tasks at high speed. A worker at a call centre must be able not only to do the job but also must complete each task within a stated time and meet hourly targets of calls answered.

Self-Help Strategies for Reading, Writing, Getting Organised and Improving Memory.

It is virtually impossible to find a job which does not require some level of reading, writing and remembering, or some use of the computer. The following section offers some tips which might help people with dyslexia in their work. These strategies, and many more, can be developed more fully by working with a specialist tutor. The topics are also covered in greater detail by a number of books and websites. Useful resources are:

- **Making Dyslexia Work for You: A Self-Help Guide** – by V. Goodwin and B. Thomson, 2004, David Fulton Publishers. ISBN 978-1843120919.

- **Dyslexia in the Workplace** – by D. Bartlett and S. Moody, 2000, Whurr Publishers. ISBN 978-1861561725.

- **The Mind Map Book: Radiant Thinking** – by T. Buzan, 2000, BBC Books, ISBN 978-0563537328.

Reading
You might read for pleasure, say a novel or a newspaper. You can read at your own pace and it doesn't matter whether you know all the words, or remember all the details.

Reading for work, or study, is another story. It is important to get the facts right, to remember the relevant information and understand what the writer is saying. If you have a lot of material to read it makes sense to:

- ✓ Get comfortable – have the right light and a quiet place.
- ✓ Have pencils, highlighters, notebooks and any other aids you need to hand.
- ✓ If you need reference books or dictionaries have them on your desk too. Searching for materials damages your concentration.
- ✓ Never sit down to read a book or document without asking yourself just why you are reading and what information you want to get.
- ✓ Skim through, looking at chapter headings and summaries.
- ✓ If an executive summary of a report is included, read it first.
- ✓ Look for the key ideas and underline with pencil or highlighter.
- ✓ Stop from time to time and ask yourself what you have just read.
- ✓ Read for 20 – 30 minutes and then take a short break. It is difficult to concentrate effectively for more than 30 minutes without a break.
- ✓ Review what you have read by making your own short summary.
- ✓ Pretend you are giving a talk on what you have read.
- ✓ Check back to make sure that you have got your facts right.

There is a well known method for reading which encapsulates the above tips and it is easy to remember because it is called SQ3R. This method, which was first developed by Francis Robinson in the 1960s, has been used for many years. SQ3R stands for Scan, Question and 3 R's – Read, Remember, Review.

Scan – look through the text quickly for key words, not ignoring any illustrations, diagrams or graphs. Important information is often highlighted in a text box or in bold or italics.
Question – ask yourself what information you hope to get from your reading.
Read – read the text fully.
Remember – write down the main points.
Review – read again to check if you have remembered correctly.

If you need to remember what you have read in great detail, say for an examination, it may help to read aloud and tape the material. Then it can be replayed as often as you like at any convenient time.

If you read quite easily but still have problems with new or uncommon words, it might be worth while buying a Reading Pen, which will scan a word, say it aloud and explain what it means. You will find more information on this pen in Chapter 9.

If you find looking up the meanings of new words in a dictionary very time consuming, it could be easier to use the Thesaurus facility on your computer.

If you find that reading black print on a white background causes you visual stress, causes the print to move or gives you a headache, you could experiment with colour filters. Using clear plastic sheets in different colours could filter the light and make print clearer for you. An alternative is to photocopy reading material on to coloured paper. If any of these strategies helps, then use them.

Some readers with dyslexia find that they skip words or lines and find it hard to keep their place on the page. Use of a bookmark, such as the x-mark (www.xmark.no) may be helpful. This bookmark comes in various colours which may also help to focus the reader on the print.

Writing
Next to reading aloud, writing is probably the activity most disliked by adults with dyslexia. Even when the writing load would seem to be a minor part of the job it can make life very difficult. Cindy worked for a time on the food counter of a pub. She recalls:

"I had to write down the orders and the menu on the blackboard outside. The office crowd would come in, suited and booted, looking down their noses at me and giving out when I got the orders wrong, which was quite a lot".

Cindy moved jobs frequently, so that "looking for a job again actually became a job in itself" until she found her niche in a driving school.

> "I loved it. The buzz of people coming and going all day, people so stressed about their driving lessons and their test that they never noticed how I spelt their names and addresses.
> Job heaven for a person with dyslexia."

Writing down names and addresses can be tricky for people with dyslexia. Phil, a receptionist who has handled her dyslexic difficulties very well, keeps a note pad on which she asks people to write down their names and addresses. She explains that she has dyslexia and adds with a smile that she would hate to get the name wrong. She says she very rarely gets a bad reaction. When on the phone, Phil mentions that she has dyslexia and asks callers to spell out their names.

Obviously, different types of writing tasks will need different levels of skill, but many can be handled with a bit of thought and creativity from the worker and flexibility on the part of management. Many letters, memos, invoices, bills, appointments, orders and acknowledgements can be dealt with by creating a template or form letter. Try, wherever possible, to have relevant words and phrases stored on your computer or written in your personal notebook, so that you can include them in correspondence. If there are words which you have trouble spelling and which you need in your work, then these can be added to your personal list.

Writing a report to present to your manager, or submitting a thesis at college can be much more challenging, but there are ways of coping.
Perhaps the hardest part is getting started.

➤ **Make a PLAN**. Do this on paper using index cards, on computer using software such as Inspiration or by making a mind map or diagram. Decide what you want to say.

➤ **Set deadlines** for yourself. If a report is due on May 31st you need to work backwards from that date and plan when you need to have a first draft ready, when you need to begin research and how much time you can spend each day on this report.

➤ **Allot time** for reading and research; time for writing; time for consultation with relevant others; time for revision; time for printing and time for unforeseen events such as computer or printer breakdown. Write your plan down on a time sheet and stick to it.

➤ **Organise your thoughts.** Reports or essays have a recognised format:
1. Introduction – tell the reader what you are going to say.
2. Discussion – set out your point of view.
3. Presentation of facts - back up your argument using examples or quotes.
4. Conclusion – tell the reader what you think is the issue.
5. Recommendations – what do you think should be done.
6. References – if you have quoted other reports or texts, it is important to list them, noting the relevant pages.

A variation of this format will give you a structure on which to write your essay or report. When you break a job down into separate parts it becomes easier. You can take one bit at a time. Start with even one sentence for each idea. You can expand on it later. Don't worry about spelling or grammar at this stage. That can be checked later using the spelling and grammar check on your computer.

If a particular section is hard to write, try talking it out – to a friend or on tape. Do remember though, that written language is more formal than spoken language, so you can't simply write as you speak.

The most important thing when writing a report or essay is not to get bogged down in one part. If one aspect or part of your argument is difficult, go on to another one. Keep going. Do not write the introduction over and over again until it is perfect, and then find you don't have time for the rest of the report. Many good writers leave the introduction to the end: it is the last thing they write.

Check carefully from time to time that you are sticking to the topic and not going off into other issues.

If your computer has a facility for converting text to voice, use this to edit your written work. For those with a good ear, it is easier to detect mistakes when you hear them, than when you read from the screen or paper.

Take extra care with words which the spell checker won't correct, e.g. 'their' for 'there' or 'wait' for 'weight'. It is a great help to get a friend or colleague to proof read your written work. However, sometimes people with dyslexia place too much pressure on themselves to have perfect spelling, so remember that everyone makes mistakes when writing or typing, not just people with dyslexia!

Memory

It is often said that with dyslexia it is not so much that people learn slowly but that they forget quickly. It is true that people with dyslexia often struggle to remember names, dates, and facts. Stress and anxiety can make this difficulty worse. Most people will recall the panic they felt as a child being asked a question in mental arithmetic, or spelling when an immediate response was required. The greater the effort made the further away the answer seemed to drift.

Memory is very complex and we have different memory ability for different stimuli. Some people with dyslexia have very good visual memory and poor auditory memory, so they will remember information better if it is presented with diagrams and visual images.
Other people with dyslexia may have poor visual memory and good auditory memory, so they will find it easier to remember what they hear, rather than what they see. People who are more kinaesthetic or active learners will remember better by practicing and doing an activity, rather than just reading about it or looking at it.

There are two main types of memory relating to the length of recall, but for facts and figures we usually need two in particular: short-term and long-term. Short-term memory is used when you hold a fact, say a phone number, in your head long enough to use it. By the following day, you no longer recall it, or need to recall it.

Long-term memory has two parts. Episodic memory is used to recall events which happened, e.g. a holiday by the sea as a child. Semantic memory is used to remember facts and details, e.g. your PPS number or the date of the Battle of Clontarf. The vital one for study and work is the semantic memory.

There are many ways for getting information into long-term memory. As a person with dyslexia it is important to work out the best way for you. Once a fact is in the long-term memory it must also be easily retrieved. The memory can be like a spare room, or attic, where things are stored in an untidy heap. Ideally it should be like a filing cabinet where each fact is neatly labelled and can be taken out when needed. But we don't live in an ideal world and much time and energy is spent in trying to recall things which we are sure we know.

The following tips may be helpful for learning and remembering information:

- **Choose the right time of day** when you know your memory is at its best. For some it's early, for others it's just before bedtime.
- **Choose the right place** – comfortable and free from distractions.

- **Link facts to other details you already have stored, or which interest you.** For example you may have enjoyed the film "West Side Story". This could be used to help remember the plot and characters in "Romeo and Juliet".
- **Make links for yourself,** e.g. your bank PIN might be 2375, you could remember "I was 23 when I first visited London and my friend Betty lives at 75 Main Street".
- **Store information in small chunks,** it is easier to remember than in large units, e.g. break a phone number into sections rather than trying to learn it whole.
- **Use mnemonics, a rhyme or phrase which helps you remember something.** For example remembering the verse "30 days hath November, April, June and September" could help you avoid the embarrassment of making appointments for April 31st. Make up your own rhymes or phrases. They can be personal, funny or even rude.
- It is very hard to remember things which you don't understand so it's worth taking some time to make sure you are fully familiar with what you want to memorise.
- **It is easier to remember things which are unusual,** so focus on any odd or interesting features.
- **Attach colours or pictures to information** if that works for you. You could highlight facts or key words in different colours and then visualise the page with the different colours.

- **Draw a mind map or diagram showing the key ideas;** you may find that you can visualise the map and retrieve the information more easily (see Figure 1).
- **Most importantly revise the information you want to remember.** If you don't, you may forget most of it within a few days.

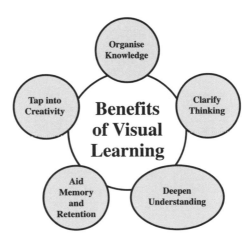

Figure 1.

People with dyslexia are often very creative in working out strategies which work for them. One mathematics student with dyslexia who found formulas hard to remember would revise them just before entering the examination hall. He would hold them in his memory until he was given his answer papers when he would jot them down immediately. He did this before reading the exam questions so as not to forget or become confused. When he read through the exam questions he would know which formulas he needed to use and he would have them to hand.

Mobile phones are a real boon to adults with dyslexia, as names, addresses, phone numbers and other brief details can be kept to hand. However, there are some facts which are almost impossible for people with dyslexia to remember and many people just give up trying. This applies particularly to multiplication tables and mathematical formulas. Once school days are over there is often no reason for most people to have to remember these and calculators, number squares, ready reckoners and slide rules provide an easy answer. Many mobile phones now include a calculator.

Many people with dyslexia carry their own personal notebooks where they record information which they find hard to remember and which they need often. This can be used to record spellings which are tricky, technical expressions, names and contact details of customers, or lists of things they have to do.

People who have trouble with remembering letters in sequence, as in filing or consulting a dictionary or telephone directory find it useful to keep an index card with the letters of the alphabet clearly written on it. This enables them to check quickly whether 'J' comes before or after 'K', a very important piece of information when you are looking for a file in a hurry.

In work and when studying it may be useful to make your own list of frequently used words, whether on index cards or on your computer.

Organisation and Time Management

Margaret Thatcher, when Prime Minister of Britain, is reported to have said "Happiness is a ticked off list."
Many people would agree. Getting things done and finished with, crossing them off the list so you don't have to worry about them any more is a great feeling.

For many workers with dyslexia the reality is that bad feelings can be more common than good ones at the end of the day. Work mounts up, pressure builds from managers or colleagues, files go missing, hastily written material contains spelling and other mistakes and very hardworking people can appear to be careless or incompetent. A small forest has been destroyed to produce paper for all the books and magazine articles on how to organise your life and manage your time. At the risk of adding to this mountain of information, here are some strategies for getting organised:

- Be like Margaret Thatcher – make a list.
- Better still, make a couple of lists.
- Write down everything you need to do today for work.
- Write down everything you need to do today for yourself.
- You could divide your daily diary into two columns, one for work and one for personal items.
- Put a red mark beside all the really urgent items, e.g. if you have to go to a meeting, or take your child to the dentist then it has to be done today. This is urgent.
- Make sure you know what is urgent for you and what is important.
- Do not spend time deleting old files on your computer when a report is required for tomorrow's meeting. That may be important but it is not urgent.
- Review your "To Do" list twice a day – at lunchtime and before going home.
- Update your list when a new task arises, otherwise you may forget it.
- Enjoy crossing off the tasks you completed at the end of the day.
- At the end of the day start your new list for tomorrow with the tasks you didn't do today.
- Keep a diary with all your appointments. Don't have two diaries with some appointments in each. It is not easy to concentrate on a demanding job at work if you have an uneasy feeling that it's your turn to collect your child from school but you are not sure.

- ✓ Get into the habit of checking your diary every morning, and again at lunch time. It is surprising how many people with dyslexia forget about appointments.
- ✓ Put a year planner on your wall in a prominent place.
- ✓ Mark in holidays, birthdays and important dates such as meetings, deadlines for projects etc. on it and look at it often.
- ✓ Use post-it notes if you find them helpful but try to reserve them for reminding yourself of unusual or very urgent things. A forest of post-it notes on your desk or wall can be confusing rather than helpful.
- ✓ Try to keep your files and paper under control.
- ✓ Try to get by with three paper trays on your desk, one labeled "Do Today", one labeled "Do Soon" and one labeled "Filing".
- ✓ Be ruthless about disposing of unwanted paper – either file it or bin it.
- ✓ The filing tray should be emptied every Friday.

 It is worth remembering that sometimes when you feel overwhelmed with work it is because you are overwhelmed. The workload is too great for any one person. People with dyslexia often feel that any difficulty they encounter is their fault and that others would cope better. If you find yourself in this situation do talk to a colleague or friend and approach your manager or employer about possibly adjusting your workload.

Chapter 7
Dyslexia – the human factor

People with dyslexia are, first and foremost, people. They are all unique persons who differ in age, size, height, personality, ability, experience, family background and life history. However, they do share some common difficulties which arise, in large part, from living in a predominantly non-dyslexic environment.

Many people with dyslexia find dealing with the written word quite tiring. This is true for children at school and for adults in the workplace. It has to be acknowledged and allowances made for it. It is important, therefore, for people with dyslexia to be aware of the role diet, exercise and relaxation can play in how they feel and how they cope with day to day activities.

A balanced diet with plenty of fresh fruit and vegetables makes good sense for anyone, but particularly for a person under stress. Medical opinion indicates that a varied diet should provide all the nutrients a person needs without resort to supplements, unless recommended by a doctor. Likewise ensuring a good night's sleep is also important.

It is a well known fact that errors of all sorts are more common when one is tired, stressed or run down. Dehydration can impair attention and concentration levels, so always have a bottle of water at your desk to keep hydrated. When studying or working on a difficult task which requires detailed attention, it is important to take a break every 20 or 30 minutes.

Many people with dyslexia find that it is difficult to work quickly and accurately when doing clerical work. In general, accuracy is the most desired aim, so speed may have to be sacrificed slightly.

The benefit of relaxation exercises should not be overlooked. Simply pausing to take a few deep breaths can be immensely helpful when feeling overwhelmed by work or study. There are many classes, tapes and books available on relaxation techniques which can really help in managing stress. Physical activity, even taking a short walk, can help to relieve stress and clear your head. Many people find activities such as yoga and martial arts not only help to develop motor skills and balance but can also aid concentration and help with relaxation.

Self-Confidence
A side-effect of dyslexia, in all too many people, is the damage to their self-confidence. Lack of confidence in their ability to do a job or take on a challenge is probably the greatest burden many adults with dyslexia have to bear. Even when initial literacy difficulties have been overcome and an individual appears secure and competent, self doubt can lurk just beneath the

surface. A set-back at work, a criticism from someone in authority, a perceived failure in achieving a goal, could reawaken memories of the classroom and shatter self-confidence.

It is unfortunately true that a lot of damage to self-confidence happens in the classroom. Frances recalls:

> "What I learned in school was not a lot. It was not much on education. I learned to have fear, and I also learned to have no confidence. Having no confidence stopped me from doing a lot of things in school, from talking and mixing with the rest of the class. I would always sit at the back of the class. This was the only comfort I had."

It took Frances many years to regain her confidence. Self-confidence is a delicate plant. It is easily stamped out but quite hard to grow again. Yet self-confidence is the key to success in so many ways.

Adults who return to education must have their self-confidence restored in order for tuition and training to be effective. Some people with dyslexia have been so hurt by their past experiences that professional counselling is necessary before they are able to tackle the underlying literacy difficulty and begin to learn. For others, understanding their lack of confidence and adopting some strategies to restore it may suffice.

Self-Esteem

Lack of self-confidence can be an enormous handicap for an adult with dyslexia faced with new and difficult tasks. However, lack of self-esteem is a more fundamental difficulty and can affect every aspect of life. Low self-esteem means that the person does not value themselves as a human being deserving of respect and fulfillment.

Most feelings of low esteem or feeling bad about oneself stem from early experiences. Factors which lead to low self-esteem include:

- Failure, or perceived failure, to be as good as everyone else.
- Lack of approval, appreciation, praise or affection.
- Punishment for failure, e.g. ridicule, exclusion, bullying.
- Being different, the odd one out – at school or at home.
- Belonging to a group which is not socially valued.

Looking at this list it is clear that adults with dyslexia could have experienced one or more of those risk factors. Even if neither parents nor teachers were explicit in criticising the child's performance, a child who underperformed in a classroom situation would have been well aware of the fact. The Irish education and child rearing culture, particularly in the past, tended to concentrate on correcting errors rather than on praising effort. Pupils were more likely to be told "you got 5 spellings wrong out of 10" rather than "you got 5 spellings right". An adult who had specific learning difficulties while in the classroom, and whose parents and teachers either had never heard of dyslexia, or did not have the resources to provide appropriate support, would almost certainly suffer huge damage to his/her self-esteem.

While the causes of low self-esteem may lie in childhood experiences, the results persist well into adulthood. Thinking poorly of oneself becomes a habit, and the longer the habit persists the more difficult it is to change. A lot has been written about ways to improve self-esteem. **Some of the following may be helpful to anyone who feels their own confidence could to with a boost:**

Give yourself credit.
You may have had some difficulties at school or in work, but then everyone does to some extent or other. The fact that you persisted and that you are now reading this booklet means you have succeeded very well indeed.

Think of what you have achieved rather than what you have not achieved. Think of the things you can do: driving a car; cooking meals; keeping to a budget; swimming; playing sport; rearing children; caring for others; keeping pigeons; volunteering in your community; drawing; decorating your home; earning a living; making friends; playing an instrument; using a computer. If you think about it you can probably add a lot more skills to that list. If you have even some of these skills you are doing well. You don't have to be brilliant at every activity. You don't have to be an Olympic swimmer, or a rally driver. These people are few and far between. Be proud of what you can do and value yourself.

Think of the courage you have shown in your life. It probably took courage to go to school every day when learning was a real challenge for you. If you returned to education as an adult, or took extra courses, or learned to use a computer, then this took great courage and determination. If you have told friends and colleagues about your dyslexia, or explained to employers or supervisors just what dyslexia means, then you have shown real courage. It is really important to give yourself credit for all you have done and all you have achieved.

Don't be your own worst critic
There is a big difference between being realistic about your own difficulties, and being constantly self-critical. It is good to be aware of what you find hard to do and it is only sensible to ask for help when necessary. But there is no advantage at all in beating yourself up for every little mistake you make. You wouldn't say a friend was useless, or a waste of space, because they found something difficult or made a mistake. Yet you do it to yourself all the time. You wouldn't write off a friend because he or she had one area of difficulty. You would see all the other positive things about that person. Could you imagine criticizing a friend because she couldn't swim, or because she failed her driving test? Why should you be so much harder on yourself?

Don't expect the worst

If your self-esteem is low you may be reluctant to take on a challenge, or try something new. You may fear that it won't work out.

Anticipating failure can really hold you back. It is more useful to concentrate your attention on what you want to achieve, rather than thinking of what might go wrong. There is a danger of over-estimating the difficulties, or worrying about what will happen if you don't succeed.

Don't dwell on the past

Everyone makes mistakes. If you spend too much time thinking about what you did wrong, you miss the chance to learn from mistakes and move on.

Trust yourself

If you are aware of your own strengths and weaknesses then you are dealing with facts. When others make assumptions about you they are dealing with opinions. A particular teacher may have considered you a failure because you didn't answer questions quickly enough. This was not a failure on your part, but was a result of the teacher's unrealistic expectations of a student with dyslexia. Consider that other people's opinions about you may be wrong. Believe in yourself and value your own knowledge of yourself. Don't compare yourself to other people. Concentrate on improving your own performance. You are the important person.

Be positive

If you allow yourself to dwell on thoughts of your difficulties, past failures, disappointments, frustrations, anxieties and even unfair treatment you received, you could easily become depressed. It is important to do something to change your mood and lift your spirits. You will know best how to banish negative thoughts and cheer yourself up. It may be by listening to music, exercising, talking to a friend, going to a film or even having a hot bath.

Melanie Fennell in her book 'Overcoming Low Self-Esteem' recommends keeping a "Positives Notebook" in which you write down not just lists of your own good points, but examples of things you did which demonstrated these positive qualities. She recommends writing down three things each day. It might be something as simple as tackling a job which you had been putting off, or calling in on an elderly neighbour, or being patient with a particularly difficult customer. This will help you to focus on positive things about yourself, rather than constantly putting yourself down.

Improving your self-esteem is probably the best thing anyone with dyslexia can do for themselves. Remember the elderly gentleman who was asked by a student researcher what social class he was in, so that the appropriate box could be ticked. The older man looked him in the eye and proudly replied:

"I'm not Upper Class, or Middle Class or Working Class, but I'm First Class."

There was a man who could give lessons in self-esteem.

Chapter 8
How Employers can Help

Employer Awareness

"Employers often find themselves trying to make up for the fact that many employees, particularly older employees, have very poor levels of education. Nowadays we are familiar with the concept of specific learning difficulties, be it dyslexia, dyspraxia or attention deficit disorder. However as recently as 10 or 15 years ago these concepts were unknown to the public and poorly understood. Employers certainly did not understand the different kinds of conditions that their employees could have and this was a real barrier to engagement with such problems. Today we have much more awareness and openness to addressing them, but we are still dealing with the legacy of the past.

I would urge employers to consider the needs of those employees who may have specific learning difficulties, to ensure that they too can avail of any education and training that is made available and are not left behind.

I encourage employers to accommodate and support this strand of talent within the workforce, because without that accommodation it is hard for many to succeed. I have no doubt that…. in the future we will wonder why dyslexia was ever considered unusual."

The above quotations are from the opening address of Mr. Turlough O'Sullivan, Director General of the Irish Business and Employers Confederation (IBEC), at a conference on dyslexia in 2007. (The full text is available on www.dyslexia.ie/conference2007.htm). His words are so true. We are still dealing with the legacy of the past and many employers do not have as much awareness as their employees might wish.

Dyslexia is a hidden disability. Employers may well be wary of how such a disability will impact on an employee's work. The assumption is often made that if a person has dyslexia, then they cannot read at all. Regrettably many people still assume that dyslexia means illiteracy or possibly impaired mental functioning. Things have not changed so much since Albert Einstein lost two lecturing posts because of his erratic spelling and poor handwriting.

Legislation
Equality legislation in Ireland prohibits discrimination against people with disabilities but anecdotal evidence suggests that it is happening and employees report incidences of bullying because of their dyslexia. The facts are hard to establish, but it is unacceptable that anyone should feel vulnerable in the workplace because of difficulties which could be accommodated, if they were better understood. The **Employment Equality Acts (1998-2004)** outlaw discrimination in all areas relevant to employment. Discrimination is defined as the treatment of one person in a less favourable way than another person is, has been or should be treated. The definition of disability includes learning disorders such as dyslexia.

An employer may not discriminate on grounds of disability, but that does not mean that an employer must hire, retain or promote an employee who cannot do a particular job. However, a person with a disability may be capable of doing a job if special accommodations are made. These adaptations or provisions of technology are often not as costly as might be feared. Before the passing of the Employment Equality Act, 2004, an employer could refuse to provide facilities if the cost was more than nominal. Nominal cost was not defined.

Under the 2004 act the requirement is that the cost of accommodations must not cause a disproportionate burden on the employer. When the burden is being assessed the criteria include the costs relative to the size of the business and the resources available, the nature of any benefit experienced by any person likely to be affected by them, and any funding available from statutory bodies for adaptation. This places more of an onus on employers to consider the provision of facilities and services for employees with disabilities than the older acts did. Funding is also now available to employers from FÁS (the Workplace Equipment Adaptation Grant), which can help with the cost of any necessary workplace adaptations or equipment, such as specialist assistive technology (see Chapter 9).

The Equality Authority can be contacted at any time for informal advice on matters relating to equality and discrimination. If an employee feels he or she has been discriminated against because of their disability, they may take a complaint to the Equality Tribunal.

How Employers can Help

Employers are in an enormously powerful situation in relation to workers with dyslexia. They can influence whether the person becomes a productive and happy member of staff or whether their employee becomes a nervous, stressed-out wreck. Below are some common sense points that employers and managers might bear in mind when working with employees or colleagues with dyslexia.

- **Talk to the individual** with dyslexia and ask him/her what they need in order to do the job effectively. People with dyslexia are not all the same. They have different abilities and different needs, and after all they are best placed to say what works for them.
- **An open atmosphere** where an employee can feel confident in talking about problems and seeking solutions is the best support which can be given.
- **Provide awareness and training** to human resources personnel, line managers and colleagues on how dyslexia impacts in the workplace. Given the prevalence of dyslexia in the population the odds are extremely high that more than one person on the staff has dyslexia.
- **Be aware of dyslexia at the recruitment stage.** Ensure that your firm is not missing out on the opportunity to hire a highly productive worker because of a difficulty which could be managed relatively easily.

- **Provide adequate training.** It is worth taking the extra time to ensure that workers know exactly what the job entails. All will have learning strengths; utilise these.
- Remember that a person with dyslexia may forget easily, so be prepared to **repeat training if required.**
- Likewise, **be patient** with questions. Better to answer the same question a few times than to deal with a costly error.
- **Give clear instructions.** Verbal instructions should be given slowly and one at a time. It is useful to check back that they have been understood. Remember that dyslexia is an information processing difficulty, not just a reading delay.
- **Written instructions should be easy to read,** preferably typed in large font, in plain English and illustrated with pictures and diagrams if possible. It may help if printing is on coloured paper.
- **Give advance notice of tasks** to be done. Pressure affects performance and workers with dyslexia may feel this more than others.
- **Avoid stress if possible.** Stress is often caused by supervisors trying to hurry a worker, or looking over their shoulder constantly.
- People with dyslexia may work better in a quiet area free from other distractions.

- **Encourage good work practices** such as pre-planning for projects, keeping work schedules and time tables, breaking jobs down into manageable units, frequent reviewing of goals and progress and mutual support from colleagues.
- Do not ask an employee with dyslexia to read aloud in public without checking that they are comfortable with this.
- Remember that taking notes at a meeting may be very difficult as many people with dyslexia find it hard to listen and write at the same time.
- Do not mistake difficulty with reading, writing or remembering for stupidity or laziness.
- Coping with dyslexia in the workplace may be difficult for an employer or supervisor, but just imagine what it is like for the employee.
- **Don't focus only on the difficulties.** People with dyslexia have many strengths, so do give praise and encouragement.

Become aware of dyslexia.
It is a fact of working life. 6% to 8% of the workforce is affected by dyslexia to some extent. A dyslexic difficulty may explain why some workers are reluctant to keep records, write reports or even to seek promotion. It may be the reason why written work does not seem to reach the standard of presentation that would be expected from the employee's proven ability in other areas.

It may also explain difficulties with time-management and even reactions to perceived authority figures. Some adults with dyslexia, who have unhappy memories of school days, carry over the fear and resentment felt as children to authority figures in the workplace. They may be afraid of their difficulties being 'found out'.

Dealing with written language and office procedures does not always come easily to people with dyslexia. It is like an athlete running a marathon with a heavy weight attached to his/her ankles. It can be done but it is difficult and tiring. The surprising thing is how many people manage to reach the finishing post. The more an employer or manager learns about dyslexia, the easier it becomes to understand what this struggle entails. The reward for employer and employee is a more productive and happier workplace.

Take a flexible approach
Create an open environment in which employees have no fear that declaring a difficulty will result in dismissal or sidelining. If a dyslexic problem is identified, it can be taken into account. It stands to reason that a difficulty which is being covered up is much more likely to result in mistakes than one which is recognised. Colleagues can be encouraged to help each other out and share or swap tasks. Work can be allocated to suit the talents of the individual and the employer gets the best from every worker.

Look at the whole person. Reading may not be a strength but there may be many other skills and abilities which are untapped. Many people with dyslexia have great interpersonal skills and are very articulate. Others have exceptional facility with information technology. Adults with dyslexia have usually learned patience and tolerance and so make understanding trainers and instructors.

Don't make assumptions
Remember that staff with high-level qualifications can still have dyslexia and that it may affect their work, particularly if they are trying to cover up the condition. An engineer may be brilliant technically, innovative, creative and highly competent at his/her job, but not feel comfortable producing written reports or reading unseen texts aloud at meetings.

Get Specialist Help
Use the many support systems which exist. Outside specialists can provide screening and psycho-educational assessment if necessary.
Individual tuition and support for employees is available. The Dyslexia Association of Ireland offers both psycho-educational assessment and individual tuition for adults.

Avail of Technological Assistance
Consider how technology can help. Word processing packages with spell and grammar check can work wonders. Voice operated software, screen readers, scanners, mobile phones with recording memory, electronic dictionaries, talking calculators, reading

pens; electronic organizers – one or more of these may solve the problem. Detailed information is available in Chapter 9.

Consider low-tech solutions. People with dyslexia often find that increasing print size to 14 points and using a plain sans serif font (e.g. Arial, Verdana, Helvetica or Sassoon) makes text easier to read.

Changing the background colour on a computer may make a huge improvement in legibility. Photo-copying information on to coloured paper, use of colour coding, or coloured hi-lighters, and use of coloured transparent sheets to cover reading material may also help.

Presenting written information
Instructions do not always have to be given in densely printed form. Short clear sentences, in plain English and well spaced on the paper are more accessible for people with dyslexia. It helps if the same terms are used consistently, e.g. referring in one place to 'cars' and in another to 'vehicular traffic' tends to confuse. Highlight key words using bold or highlighters. Italics and underlining may confuse. Lines should be left justified only and writing in all capital letters should be avoided. Bullet points and numbers for key facts are also helpful.

A picture is worth a thousand words to a person with dyslexia. Illustrations, diagrams, flow charts and mind maps can be enormously helpful. Visual literacy is a skill not to be underestimated. Some day we may all need to have it!

Vive le Difference
A key factor in dyslexia is difference. Employers can view this difference as a positive or a negative. If a worker with dyslexia does not find a particular system, or training practice suits their learning style, ask them what would suit. There may be another way and it may even be better, not just for them but for the entire staff.

Dyslexia, Dyspraxia, Dyscalculia, ADD/ADHD and Asperger's Syndrome all make life difficult for the person with the condition. They also have implications for employers, colleagues, college authorities and examining bodies. But it must be understood that all of these conditions have their upsides.

People with Dyslexia and ADD think and process information differently. While they may experience difficulty in processing written language, they can process non-language information very efficiently. This has been an important trait in human evolution, and as Dr. Duncan Milne, says in *'Teaching the Brain to Read':*

"Having different types of problem solvers within the group is essential. By having both symmetrical and asymmetrical brains working in the same team, synergies lead to better problem solving".

Indeed this ability of many people with dyslexia (who are believed to be right brain dominant) to solve problems has led some American firms to employ only engineers with dyslexia.

In an article in Fortune Magazine (May 2002), Betsy Morris profiles some very successful business people, bankers, lawyers and entrepreneurs, all millionaires or billionaires, who succeeded in spite of major dyslexic difficulties. The best known, on this side of the Atlantic, is tycoon Richard Branson, who left school at sixteen and went on to build an aviation empire.

The author, Thomas G. West, has written in detail about the achievements of engineers, scientists and information technology innovators who have dyslexia. In Harvard, he reports, dyslexia is known as the M.I.T. (Massachusetts Institute of Technology) disease because so many of the students at this prestigious institute have the condition. Creative artists from Leonardo da Vinci to the sculptor Rodin have displayed dyslexic characteristics, as did Nobel Prize winning poet William Butler Yeats.

With all learning difficulties it is essential to develop an understanding of the individual's strengths and weaknesses, and their learning style. The strengths can be capitalized upon and used to help overcome the weaker areas.

Chapter 9
Computers and Assistive Technology

In previous chapters we have mentioned that technology can help people with dyslexia in the workplace and in their studies. There is a vast range of software and technical equipment out there, some of it geared for students' needs, but much of it suitable for any user.

Adults with dyslexia should feel free to experiment with whatever is available and search around until they find what suits them best. Needs will vary hugely, from the person who needs the simplest method of reading the written word, to the third level student who wants to edit and present formal academic texts.

It is always well to remember that technology is a tool and is not in any way a substitute for specialist teaching. It should also be borne in mind that to use technology effectively requires training. This can be time consuming, but it is pointless to spend a lot of money on sophisticated equipment unless adequate training in its best use is provided. The most appropriate equipment for each individual has to be considered and the most expensive option may not always be the best one.

Useful aids and techniques range from very simple items like coloured highlighters to expensive high tech computer programmes.

This section includes some of the things which people with dyslexia have found helpful.

Cheap and Cheerful Aids

Coloured photocopying paper - Some people find that they get less glare or experience less visual stress when reading material printed on coloured paper. Yellow is a favourite. Other options are the use of coloured overlays which are placed over the text. It is also possible to change the font colour and background colour on the computer.

Pictures, diagrams, charts and mind-maps can convey a lot of information to a person with dyslexia and save a lot of reading.

Readers who have trouble keeping their place on the page may find a simple bookmark like the X-mark helps. This guides the eye while reading and some readers find the colours help with visual stress. These are now available from the Dyslexia Association.

Post-it notes in different colours can be useful for reminders. Some students like to plan essays using post-it notes. They can be spread on a desk and moved about as required.

Coloured highlighters are useful for marking important words or phrases in a text.

A personal notebook to keep lists of words or phrases which are often needed can be useful. This is easier to manage than looking up dictionaries or reference books.

Clear plastic file folders in a variety of colours can be used to organise paper work. For example, all papers on a particular essay topic, or job of work could be kept in red folders. These will be easily identified when needed.

Colour coding files using sticky labels is also helpful.

A copy holder with a moveable ruler is very useful if work involves transcribing rows of figures, names and addresses or other closely printed text.

Spending a little more – small electronic devices.
People with dyslexia often have difficulty in listening and taking notes at the same time, so recording lectures, or training sessions can be really helpful. This can be done with a digital recorder. This means that they can replay the information as often as necessary. They can build up their own audio library which they can then use for revision and any future work which needs to be done. An MP3 player can be used so that material can be listened to at leisure or while travelling.

This strategy is also very useful in the workplace when taking minutes or writing reports on meetings. Of course, any type of recording does require the consent of lecturers and those attending meetings.

At third level some students with dyslexia are allowed to record answers to examination questions on tape. This can be a huge benefit for some students who may see their grades increase significantly as a result.

Small hand held recorders are very useful to record phone messages, orders, names and addresses, jobs to be done, etc.

An **electronic dictionary** is an inexpensive, portable tool for checking spelling, e.g. Franklin Spellmaster. As long as the individual can make a reasonable phonetic attempt, there is a good chance that the correct spelling can be identified. Some electronic dictionaries also have a thesaurus feature which can help with expanding vocabulary.

Electronic organisers are invaluable for storing relevant information, phone numbers, addresses, diary entries. They can be set to remind one of appointments and meetings.

Modern mobile phones will now do many of the above tasks.

High-tech Options
Developments in computers and assistive technology have been of great benefit to people with dyslexia, both as students and in the workplace. Access to even a basic word processor with spell and grammar check is a

big help. Checking spelling on computer is so much easier than consulting a dictionary and the thesaurus function makes looking up word meanings quicker and simpler.

Good keyboard skills are essential, so it is important to learn proper touch-typing. Scanners, which allow text to be put directly onto a computer, and screen reading software which reads this material aloud, are extremely helpful to people who find reading tiring or difficult. Voice operated software allows the user to dictate directly onto the computer without having to worry about spelling which makes producing written work much easier and speedier.

With so many programmes and products available, it is easy to become confused with the choice. Computer software can be expensive and comes packaged, so it can be difficult to find out prior to purchase if a product is suitable. Ways of obtaining practical experience of the software include advice from other users, demonstrations of software at conferences or exhibitions; it can sometimes be possible to get free 30-day demo or trial disks from suppliers or download trial versions from the internet.

For example, the following websites offer free demos and/or downloads:
www.inspiration.com   www.spark-space.com
www.clarosoftware.com   www.penfriend.ltd.uk
demo@texthelp.com (email)

Computer literacy is becoming necessary for everyone in the workforce and to be able to use a word processor effectively it is important to learn to touch type properly. It does take some time and effort but it is well worth it.

Developing reading, spelling and numeracy skills
While many adults will choose to deal with any literacy difficulties they still have by working with a specialist tutor, this may not be possible for everyone. There are hundreds of excellent programmes available which motivated adults can use by themselves to help to improve their basic skills in reading, spelling and maths.

Many programmes come in a range of different levels; it is important to choose the right level for each individual. Catalogues of educational software can be obtained from many of the specialist suppliers listed at the end of this section. The programmes mentioned below are some examples of the types commonly used.

There are many literacy programmes available which provide a useful learning aid to practise and develop reading, phonics, spelling, etc. **Wordshark,** based on the 'Alpha to Omega' programme, combines the fun of computer games with learning to spell and read. It offers 41 games that use sound, graphics and text to teach and reinforce word recognition and spelling. New words and vocabularies can also be added. This programme can be used by adults.

The **Lexia** reading series helps students to strengthen skills through interactive exercises working on areas such as phonemic awareness, decoding skills and comprehension.

Starspell is a programme suitable for adults who want to develop spelling skills. It uses the Look-Cover-Write-Check strategy. Every word is spoken and many have pictures. It is also possible to create personal word lists and subject specific vocabularies.

Reading support – accessing text
For students or other adults with reading difficulties, accessing serious reading material can be very difficult and time consuming. For those whose reading is reasonably competent, but where they come across occasional words that they cannot identify, a reading pen is a good solution, e.g. Quicktionary **Reading Pen.** These are hand held pens containing OCR software which enables them to scan and read words and phrases; they also include a dictionary to explain what a word means.

Adults who have more significant reading difficulty may need to go for a complete text-to-speech option, using **screen reading software**. Screen reading software will read any text on the computer screen, whether it is text which the person has just typed, an email or webpage, or pages of a textbook which have been scanned into the computer. When used together a scanner and screen reading package can make even very slow readers self-sufficient. The reading voice and reading speed can be adjusted; words can be read word-by-word, in sentences or continuous passages. Text scanned in can even be converted to an audio file format and downloaded onto an MP3 player to be listened to later.

Examples of this type of screen reading programme are **ClaroRead, Kurzweil** and **TextHelp.** ClaroRead and TextHELP have additional features supporting the production of written work, e.g. talking spell checker, homophone checkers and predictive typing. ClaroRead works closely alongside Dragon Dictate (see below) resulting in seamless dictation and proof reading of text. Mobile versions of this type of software are now available (the programme comes on a USB drive); this means that the student can carry the software with them and use it on any compatible computer.

Writing support
Access to even a basic word processing programme can be helpful, and a person with dyslexia will produce better work on a computer than if they were handwriting. The computer will always produce clear legible writing, whereas handwriting may be difficult to read. Spelling can be checked using the spellchecker.

Editing and rearranging text is easy, so users do not have to rewrite laboriously to produce a final draft. This facility also helps those who have sequencing difficulties as it is easy to edit the text so as to rearrange the sequence. Forgotten information can simply be added in later, or a paragraph moved to improve the flow of the passage.

Screen readers are also a very useful tool for supporting writing. They allow the user to hear any errors, e.g. a mis-typed word, or an incomplete sentence. ClaroRead and TextHELP also have a homophone checker; possible homonyms e.g. their/there, bare/bear, beech/beach, are identified in the text and the user is then given guidance to help identify whether they have the correct word. Both programmes also have word prediction.

Software such as **Textease, Co:Writer** and **Penfriend** support writing with features such as talking spellcheckers, which makes the choosing of the correct spelling easier, and word prediction, which can increase the speed of written production and in so doing increase the individual's confidence in their writing ability.

Voice recognition software, which was originally designed so that astronauts could use computers while tucked up in their space suits, is ideally suited for older students and adults who have to produce extended pieces of written work such as long essays. All instructions can be given verbally; the computer will type as you speak. **Dragon Naturally Speaking** is the most commonly used programme of this type. While this type of software has improved greatly over the last decade, it will rarely be 100% accurate. There is an initial training period where the programme learns about the user's voice, and the accuracy does improve with usage, as each time the programme is used it learns more about the user's voice, speech patterns and the vocabulary commonly use. A compatible digital voice recorder can be used with Dragon; this means that documents can be created by voice anywhere, and when the digital recorder is linked with the PC, Dragon can then transcribe the document.

To get the best from both screen reading and voice recognition software a **powerful, modern computer, with a good soundcard is essential;** these programmes either may not work at all or else work poorly on older machines. A good quality microphone is also important, ideally one that limits external noise which can distract or confuse the software.

Organisational and Study Skills
A very common feature of dyslexia is poor organisation skills, which affects many areas, e.g. planning, keeping deadlines, and especially the organisation of information, whether it is making notes or composing longer written passages.

Mind-mapping software programmes are very useful tools for those who are strong visual learners. Information can be converted into a visual mind-map containing key information, pictures and showing connections. Students can use mind-mapping software to create visual revision aids, but it can also be used for brainstorming, concept mapping and planning in the workplace. Inspiration is the most commonly used programme of this type.

Wordswork is a multi-sensory programme on study skills. While it was designed primarily for undergraduate students with dyslexia, it is relevant also for adults, particularly those who want to improve their skills before going back to formal education. It uses graphics, voiceovers, colour and humour to develop a variety of skills which students with dyslexia (and others) need to address. Topics covered include essay writing, memory strategies, exam revision and time management. It also includes sections on reading, spelling, grammar and other areas.

There are some programmes on the market which may help to improve memory using various interactive activities and games, e.g. Mastering Memory. They present sequences of pictures, words and symbols to be remembered, and gradually increase the difficulty level and speed.

Useful websites with information on the use of technology:

- British Educational Communications and Technology Agency (BECTA)
  www.becta.co.uk

- British Dyslexia Association (BDA)
  www.bdadyslexia.org.uk

- iAnsyst Ltd. (Texthelp)
  www.dyslexic.com

Major Special Needs Software Publishers
Most of their software can be bought from the suppliers listed below.

Crick Software	www.cricksoft.com
Don Johnston	www.donjohnston.com
Inclusive Technology Ltd.	www.inclusive.co.uk
Inspiration Software	www.inspiration.com
Riverdeep Learning	www.riverdeep-learning.co.uk
Semerc	www.semerc.com
Sherston	www.sherston.com

Specialist Suppliers

A wide variety of software and hardware catalogues are available from the suppliers listed below:

Award Systems, 38 Pine Valley Park,
Grange Road, Dublin 16.
Tel: 01 4930011
Website: www.awardsys.net

Diskovery, Unit 2, Waveney,
Howth Harbour, Co. Dublin.
Tel: 01 8063910
Website: www.diskovery.ie

Easy PC, Unit M7, Smithtown Industrial Estate,
Shannon, Co. Clare.
Tel. 061 719537
Website: www.easypc.ie

iAnsyst Ltd., Fen House, Fen Road, Chesterton,
Cambridge CB4 1UN, England.
Tel. 0044 1223 420101
Website: www.dyslexic.com

Jackson Technology, 24 Kiltipper Avenue,
Aylesbury, Dublin 24.
Tel: 01 4518508 and 01 4624793
Website: www.jacksontechnology.com

Scanning Pens Ltd., 6 The Quadrant, Newark
Close, Royston SC85HL, England.
Tel: 0044 87 07203310
Website: www.scanningpens.co.uk

TextHelp Systems Ltd., Enkalon Business Centre,
25 Randalstown Road, Antrim,
B41 4LJ Northern Ireland.
Tel: 048 84942810
Website: www.texthelp.com

Appendix A: The Dyslexia Association of Ireland

The Dyslexia Association of Ireland (DAI) has been working with individuals with dyslexia for over thirty years. Its aim is to provide information, advice, assessment, tuition and support to people with dyslexia.

DAI is a company limited by guarantee that has charity status. It has an office at Suffolk Chambers, 1 Suffolk Street, Dublin 2 and branches all around the country. See the website **www.dyslexia.ie** for details of branches. Membership of the DAI is open to any interested person and the fee is €40 per year (reduced rates available for people on low income).

Psycho-educational assessment for adults is available at the office in Dublin. The cost in 2009 is €400.00. Some funding is available for people who cannot afford the fee, i.e. those on social welfare or on very low incomes. Please do ask if you need assistance with the fee.

Lists of teachers who are qualified to work with adults with dyslexia can be supplied to members of the association who have been diagnosed as having dyslexia.

DAI sponsors a full-time course for unemployed adults with dyslexia. This course is administered by FÁS and is supported by a grant from the Further Education section of the Department of Education and Science. The course is called Career Paths for People with Dyslexia and is takes place in Celbridge, Co. Kildare. Further information is available from DAI at 01 6790276, or from the Career Paths Office, 01 6270805 or from any FÁS office. The course number to quote for FÁS enquiries is AT58F.

DAI also provides training courses for teachers and adult literacy tutors interested in learning more about working with people with dyslexia. "Dyslexia awareness training sessions can be arranged for companies and organisations on request."

Contact details for the Dyslexia Association of Ireland:

Address: Suffolk Chambers,
1 Suffolk Street, Dublin 2.

Telephone: 01 6790276

Email: info@dyslexia.ie

Website: www.dyslexia.ie

GALWAY COUNTY LIBRARIES

Appendix B: References and Useful Resources

BOOKS

Dyslexia: An Irish Perspective – by M. Ball, A. Hughes and W. McCormack, 2006, Blackhall Publishing. ISBN 1842180959.

Dyslexia in the Workplace – by D. Bartlett and S. Moody, 2000, Whurr Publishers. ISBN 978-1861561725.

Identical Triplets with Asperger's Syndrome – by E. Burgoine and L. Wing, 1983, British Journal of Psychiatry, Vol. 143, pp 261-5.

The Mind Map Book – Radiant Thinking – by T. Buzan, 2000 edition, BBC Books. ISBN 978-0563537328.

The Asperger Social Guide: How to Relate to Anyone in any Social Situation as an Adult with Asperger's Syndrome – by G. Edmonds and D. Worton, 2006, Chapman Educational Publishing. ISBN 978-1412920247.

Overcoming Low Self-esteem – by M. Fennell, 1999, Robinson Publishers. ISBN 978-1854877253.

Making Dyslexia Work for You: A Self-Help Guide (with CD) – by V. Goodwin and B. Thomson, 2004, David Fulton Publishers. ISBN 978-1843120919.

Overcoming Dyslexia – by B. Morris, 2002. Article in Fortune Magazine.

Adult Dyslexia: Assessment, Counselling and Training – by D. McLoughlin, G. Fitzgibbon and V. Young, 1994, Whurr Publishers.
ISBN 1897635354.

The Adult Dyslexic: Interventions and Outcomes – by D. McLoughlin, C. Leather and P. Stringer, 2002, Whurr Publishers.
ISBN 1861560451.

Teaching the Brain to Read – by D. Milne, 2002, SK Publishing.
ISBN 0958256136.

Dyslexia in Adults: Education and Employment – by G. Reid and J. Kirk, 2001, Wiley Publishers. ISBN 0471852058.

A.D.D. on the Job: Making Your A.D.D. Work for You – by L. Weiss, 1996, Taylor Trade Publishing.
ISBN 978-0878339174.

In the Mind's Eye – by T.G. West, 1997, Prometheus Books.
ISBN 978-1573921558.

Useful Websites:

www.dyslexia.ie — Dyslexia Association of Ireland

www.ahead.ie — Association for Higher Education Access and Disability

www.education.ie — Deptartment of Education & Science

www.fas.ie — FÁS

www.ncge.ie — National Council for Guidance in Education

www.nala.ie — National Adult Literacy Agency

www.nln.ie — National Learning Network

www.bda-dyslexia.org — British Dyslexia Association

www.adult-dyslexia.org — Adult Dyslexia Organisation